the**disciplinary interview**

ALAN FOWLER

Alan Fowler has worked widely in both the private and public sectors, with personnel appointments in four industries and two local authorities. He is now a freelance consultant, a director of Personnel Publications Ltd, and a member of the editorial board of *People Management*, the bimonthly journal of the CIPD. He has written widely on personnel issues, with regular articles in *People Management* and the *Local Government Chronicle*. His books include (in the *Management Shapers* series) *Negotiating, Persuading and Influencing* (1995) and *Writing Job Descriptions* (1997); and *Get More – and More Value – from Your People* (1998) and *Get More – and More Results – from Your People* (1998) – all published by the CIPD.

Management Shapers is a comprehensive series covering all the crucial management skill areas. Each book includes the key issues, helpful starting points and practical advice in a concise and lively style. Together, they form an accessible library reflecting current best practice – ideal for study or quick reference.

The Chartered Institute of Personnel and Development is the leading publisher of books and reports for personnel and training professionals, students, and all those concerned with the effective management and development of people at work. For full details of all our titles, please contact the Publishing Department:

tel. 020-8263 3387
fax 020-8263 3850
e-mail publish@cipd.co.uk

The catalogue of all CIPD titles can be viewed on the CIPD website:
www.cipd.co.uk/publications

the**disciplinary interview**

ALAN FOWLER

Chartered Institute of Personnel and Development

First published in the *Training Extras* series in 1996

First published in the *Management Shapers* series in 1998
Reprinted 2001

Typesetting by Paperweight
Printed in Great Britain by
The Guernsey Press, Channel Islands

British Library Cataloguing in Publication Data
A catalogue record for this book is available from the
British Library

ISBN
0-85292-753-3

Chartered Institute of Personnel and Development, CIPD House,
Camp Road, London SW19 4UX
Tel.: 020 8971 9000   Fax: 020 8263 3333
E-mail: cipd@cipd.co.uk   Website: www.cipd.co.uk
Incorporated by Royal Charter. Registered charity no. 1079797

contents

Other titles in the series:

1 the disciplinary interview in context

Employees who are required to attend a disciplinary interview will understandably approach the meeting with considerable trepidation. As a manager, you will also be aware that conducting such interviews can be similarly stressful. What may well have been a friendly working relationship with one of your staff is now set aside in a formal event which may have serious employment consequences for the employee, or difficult legal outcomes for the organisation. Emotions can run high, your views may be challenged, and you may have to react quickly to facts or arguments that you have not previously considered.

Potential pitfalls

There are a number of potential pitfalls in the conduct of the disciplinary interview; it is worthwhile being aware of these as a precursor to the main theme of this book – how to conduct disciplinary interviews effectively. The most common faults are:

- failing to keep an open mind about the employee's offence until you have heard all the evidence

- losing control of the interview and allowing it to degenerate into a bad-tempered argument

▲   reacting defensively to any criticisms the employee may make about you or the organisation

◉   treating the interview simply as a quasi-judicial matter of establishing guilt or innocence, and overlooking its potential contribution to improvements in conduct, attitude, or performance

◉   failing to distinguish between misconduct, for which disciplinary sanctions may be appropriate, and poor performance, which may be the result of inadequate training or poor supervisory guidance

◉   failing to give the employee an adequate opportunity to put his or her case, or forgetting to consider mitigating factors

◼   being inconsistent in the standards or decisions you apply to similar cases

▲   failing to keep an adequate record of the interview, thus causing problems at an appeal stage or if the case goes to an industrial tribunal.

Potential opportunities

Effective handling of the disciplinary interview is not just a matter of avoiding these faults: there is a more positive aspect. Handled well, disciplinary interviews can:

◉   help to explain and secure high standards of conduct and performance

■ demonstrate to all employees that the organisation acts fairly and consistently in maintaining these standards

▲ help employees to improve their performance or conduct and thus enhance their value to the organisation and their own employability

● identify and correct issues that may be undermining staff morale

● promote your organisation's values

● enhance your reputation as an effective manager – both with your own staff and with senior management.

Before considering the detailed planning and conduct of the disciplinary interview, it is important to set it within two contexts: its place within your organisation's overall disciplinary policy and procedure; and its conformity to a set of principles about good practice which have become established through case law.

Your organisation's disciplinary policy

It is a statutory requirement for employees to be notified in writing of the disciplinary rules that apply to them, and all but very small organisations possess documented disciplinary policies and procedures. ACAS (the independent advisory and conciliation service) has also published a disciplinary code of practice and related guidance material on the subject. Although the detail of procedures varies from organisation to organisation, all have three main stages:

- a disciplinary enquiry or investigation to determine the facts and decide whether further action is necessary

- if indicated by the investigation, a disciplinary interview or hearing (the subject of this book)

▲ an appeal procedure.

It is important to distinguish between the first two stages and, if possible, for each to be handled by a different person. Suppose, for example, that a supervisor reports to you that one of her employees has been rude towards a customer, despite earlier informal warnings about similar conduct. The supervisor asks you to initiate formal disciplinary action. If, in your organisation's procedure, you are the manager who would have to conduct the formal disciplinary interview, it would be helpful if you could depute someone else to make the initial investigation. For example, you might ask your personnel officer to obtain statements for you from the supervisor, the customer, and any relevant witnesses. You could then assess whether it would be appropriate to proceed with the formal disciplinary interview. Having someone else carry out the preliminary investigation prevents possible criticism that, if you not only investigate but also interview, you are acting as judge and jury.

Of course, there may be circumstances in which it is either impracticable or unnecessary to delegate the investigation. In small organisations there may be no one else to whom the investigation can be devolved. Or you may be the direct and only observer of the employee's conduct. But some initial investigation is always necessary.

Whether or not you conduct these enquiries yourself, it is important that they are thorough, but are restricted to finding the facts. Thus if the complaint against the employee is persistent lateness, the enquiry should establish the precise details of the attendance record. The employee's explanations and the supervisor's comments are a matter for the subsequent disciplinary interview. Remember that case law has defined a fair dismissal as one in which there has been a sufficient investigation to sustain a genuine belief in the employee's 'guilt'. Although many disciplinary interviews do not result in dismissal, the same principle of reaching decisions only after a thorough investigation still applies.

Case law principles

The influence of case law is not restricted to the requirement to show the adequacy of any investigation. It also affects the disciplinary interview itself. There are four key principles:

1   The employee must be told that the interview is a *disciplinary* interview and that it is in accordance with the organisation's documented disciplinary procedure. It is unfair – at law and in practice – to call an employee to a disciplinary interview without explaining its disciplinary status.

2   The employee must also be told in advance what the complaint or 'charge' is that will be the subject of the interview, and be given sufficient notice of the interview to prepare a response.

3   At the interview, the employee must be given an adequate opportunity to provide an explanation.

4   The employee should be given the facility to be accompanied by a helper – usually a shop steward in a unionised organisation, or a colleague.

The appeal procedure

Case law (and the ACAS code) also requires employees subject to dismissal to have the opportunity of an appeal to a senior manager. You need to bear this in mind if there is choice between your holding a disciplinary interview or delegating this to one of your staff. If you are the manager to whom an appeal might be made, you should not conduct the interview, because it is a breach of natural justice both to make a decision to dismiss and to hear an appeal against your own decision. In very small organisations there may however be no alternative to combining these two roles, and the courts have recognised this. But in the vast majority of cases, the disciplinary interview and any appeal should be conducted by different managers.

Remember, too, that one of the grounds for an appeal may be that the disciplinary interview was not conducted either fairly or in accordance with the organisation's established procedure. Setting the interview in its proper place within this procedure, handling it in accordance with the legally established principles, and keeping a record to assist in any later appeal or industrial tribunal hearing are all part of the effective management of discipline.

Your organisation's disciplinary procedure

Are you confident you know about your organisation's disciplinary procedure? Use the table on pages 8–9 to check for any elements you are not sure of.

Disciplinary questionnaire

Does your organisation's formal disciplinary procedure:

	Yes	No	Not sure
1 require an investigation before the disciplinary interview?			
2 specify that this investigation must be carried out by someone other than the manager conducting the interview?			
3 give employees a completely free choice as to whom they may wish to have to help or to represent them at the interview?			
4 specify (if the answer to no. 3 is 'no') who may be excluded (eg a solicitor)?			
5 require the employee to notify you in advance of any representative and/or witnesses they wish to attend?			
6 require you to notify the employee of those who will be present at the interview?			

(continued opposite)

	Yes	No	Not sure
7 require more than one manager to be present at the interview?			
8 specify a procedure for the interview?			
9 specify the form in which a record of the interview should be made?			
10 specify that managers hearing appeals must not be those who conducted the interview?			
11 limit employees's appeal rights in any way (eg appeals permitted only for dismissals)?			

2 preparing for the interview

Just as for selection or appraisal interviewing, the disciplinary interview needs thorough preparation. You need only refer back to the potential pitfalls outlined in Chapter 1 to see the risks of plunging into an interview without being clear about the procedure or the objectives. This is particularly important if feelings are running high as a result of the events that triggered the interview. Many employers have lost tribunal cases through disciplinary action taken in the heat of the moment which failed to comply with their own procedures or was in conflict with the principles established by case law. There are four main elements to consider before the interview is held:

1   ensuring all the relevant facts and documents will be available

2   deciding whom to involve and the procedure to be followed

3   telling the employee about the matters to be considered at the interview, explaining how it will be conducted, and describing the employee's rights, ie to be accompanied and to call witnesses

4   deciding the practical arrangements – timing, location, recording.

Getting the facts

Chapter 1 dealt briefly with the need, in almost all cases, for some preliminary investigation to establish relevant facts. Factual information tends to fall into three categories:

1   statements by witnesses (eg of alleged misconduct). It is generally advisable for the person conducting the investigation to obtain written witness statements – or to ask witnesses to sign their agreement that notes of what they have said are accurate. (For further points about witnesses, see later in this chapter on 'the who and the how' of the interview, and Chapter 3 on the place of witnesses within the interview procedure)

2   documentary evidence, such as attendance records, cost or quality data, or copies of relevant letters or memos

3   the employee's previous employment record, particularly appraisal data and records of any previous disciplinary action or warnings.

It is also helpful to have available copies of the formal disciplinary procedure and any rules or regulations that the employee is alleged to have broken, such as safety or cash-handling regulations.

Of course, the employee or his or her representative may produce new material at the interview, including witnesses who may give a different version of events from that of the management witnesses. But this only emphasises the need for any preliminary investigation to be as thorough as possible. It undermines management credibility if, at the interview, the employee produces information that puts a completely new complexion on the situation but that could have been discovered earlier had the management investigation been more rigorous.

Once the investigation is complete, you must decide whether formal disciplinary action is appropriate. Be particularly careful about proceeding down the disciplinary path if the issue is one of poor performance rather than misconduct. If poor quality work or a failure to meet output targets is apparently the result of negligence or a refusal to carry out prescribed working procedures, disciplinary action may well be justified. But in other cases, the evidence may point to such causes as ill-health, inadequate training, or poor supervision. In such cases, it is a matter of managerial strength, not weakness, to drop disciplinary action and initiate alternative and constructive measures to help the employee improve. See also Chapter 5.

The who and how of the interview

Your organisation's disciplinary policy may define clearly *who* should conduct and be present at the interview, and *how* the interview should be conducted. If so, it is very important you follow this to the letter. Case law has established that although a dismissal may be justified by the nature of an employee's misconduct, the dismissal can nevertheless be unfair if the organisation failed to follow its own published procedure. Apart from considerations of natural justice, one reason for this is that, in almost all cases, the published procedure will have been incorporated in employees' individual contracts of employment. So to depart from this procedure amounts to a breach of contract. That is why the results of the questionnaire at the end of Chapter 1 are important.

In many organisations, however, management involvement in the interview and the interview procedure are not prescribed in any detail. In these circumstances, you will need to consider how best to proceed.

Be wary of conducting the interview on your own, unless the matter is very straightforward and unlikely to be contested by the employee. This is particularly important if the employee is accompanied by a colleague or trade union representative. If it is later alleged that you mishandled the interview, it may be your word against that of two other people – not a happy position to be in. It is also very difficult to make an adequate record of what may be a complex discussion when you are a leading participant. So ask your personnel officer or another management colleague to sit in with you and take notes.

You need also to decide whether, in putting the matters of concern to the employee, you should call relevant witnesses. As a general rule, if witness statements are a key element in the case you should require these persons to attend, so that the employee can hear at first hand what they have alleged and have the opportunity to question their statements. A typical case would involve two employees being disciplined for fighting, when each blames the other for starting the fight. If the investigation has produced statements from, say, a chargehand and another employee who witnessed the incident, they should attend the interview to say what they saw. Where customers or other persons external to the organisation are concerned, you cannot insist on their presence – nor would a tribunal expect this. Their written statements can suffice, provided you supply copies to the employee in advance of the interview.

Employees sometimes ask for management assistance in persuading reluctant colleagues to be witnesses or provide a statement in their support – and may argue that a failure to obtain such support makes the disciplinary process unfair. You may experience similar difficulties in getting employees to provide relevant evidence to support a management complaint. It is important to recognise that, unlike court proceedings, there are no formal powers to require anyone to act as a witness or give written statements, whether for you or the employee. Nor is there any legal obligation for you to provide the employee with assistance in their preparation for the interview. Bear in mind, however, that one objective is to obtain as rounded a view of the matter as possible. If it is evident that some employees have relevant knowledge but are reluctant to speak, then whether or not their potential evidence supports the initial management view it is desirable that this evidence is available at the interview. You should not coerce people into giving evidence but, by explaining the importance of the matter and reassuring them about their involvement, you may be able to overcome what is often very understandable reluctance to become involved. From a legal viewpoint, the important principle is that you do whatever is reasonably practicable to discover all the relevant facts.

Disciplinary interviews can become very confused unless they are structured. The employee may interrupt you or a witness in the course of a statement. You may be tempted to do the same in order to register your disagreement with the employee's response. The interview may then quickly degenerate into an argument in which key points may be lost and tempers frayed. Although a very rigid procedure may inhibit a constructive discussion, the following framework for the interview is one that ACAS recommend and also one that most experienced practitioners find helpful:

● The complaint against the employee is stated, either by you or by someone deputed to put the management case.

■ Any supporting witnesses give their statements.

▲ The employee and/or his or her representative are able to ask questions about these statements.

● The employee, or employee's representative, give their side of the story and may call supporting witnesses.

- You (with any management colleagues who are assisting) may then ask questions of the employee and the employee's witnesses.

- There may then be a period of more general discussion in which any further matters either you or the employee wish to raise can be considered.

- Finally, you give the employee the opportunity to highlight the aspects that he or she wishes to emphasise, and you close the meeting with your own summary.

You should then adjourn, while you consider what your final decision should be.

Informing the employee

It is obviously a breach of natural justice to summon an employee to a disciplinary interview without telling them of the nature or substance of the meeting. They must be told what the interview is about and be given sufficient notice to enable them to prepare a response. Some organisations' procedures require that the employee must be notified in writing, and specify a minimum notice period – typically three to five working days – but many leave these points for managers to decide.

In such instances, there are no rigid rules and it is a matter of exercising common-sense judgement in each case. In general, the more complex or serious the case, the more time should be allowed for the employee to prepare a response, and the more information should be supplied to the employee beforehand. Remember that the objective of disciplinary interviews is to resolve problem situations *constructively* – not to catch employees out by springing surprise allegations on them.

It is good practice to confirm the interview in writing and to use this notification to explain the nature of the matters to be considered and the procedure to be followed. An example of such a letter could read:

This letter confirms that you are required to attend a disciplinary interview in my office on (date) at (time).

At this interview, the matter to be dealt with is the complaint by your supervisor that on (date) you were rude and aggressive towards (name), a customer of the company. Your supervisor and (name), who witnessed this incident, will attend the interview, and I also enclose a copy of a statement by the customer.

At the interview you will be able to ask questions about your supervisor's and the witnesses' statements, and will then be asked to give your response to the complaints. You may also call witnesses in your support. You (and your witnesses, if any) may then be questioned. Please inform me by (date) if you wish to call any witnesses on your behalf and if so, who they are.

You are entitled, if you wish, to be accompanied by a work colleague or your trade union representative.

Practical arrangements

The effectiveness of the disciplinary interview (or that of any other kind of interview) is affected by its timing and physical setting. A common failing is to assume the matter is sufficiently simple to be dealt with in a very short time. Perhaps you allow only half an hour, with an important management meeting scheduled immediately afterwards. At the interview, the employee embarks on an unexpectedly long and complicated explanation and, with increasing impatience, you watch your half hour expiring. What do you do? The temptation is to cut the employee short so that you are not late for your next appointment. That, however, is a recipe for an allegation of unfairness. There are two guidelines to avoid this risk:

1 Allow more time for the interview than initially seems necessary. Experience indicates that these interviews are often quite protracted, and it is important that employees and their representatives are not given the impression, through managerial impatience, that the outcome is predetermined.

2 If the interview is still uncompleted when you need to attend to other work, adjourn the case part-heard and arrange to reconvene later.

Interviews need also to take place in a room where there will be no interruptions by telephone or callers. If you work in an open-plan environment, it is essential that the interview is conducted in a closed interview or conference room, and that the proceedings cannot be overheard by anyone outside. If the employee or witnesses have to wait, the waiting area should not be in full view of other employees. Confidentiality and privacy should be maintained at the highest level that the location can provide.

Reference has already been made to the need to keep a record of the interview. An accurate and unbiased summary is required, and you should ensure that whoever is present to make this record understands what is wanted. Occasionally the employee or trade union representative may ask to tape record the whole interview. Be very cautious about agreeing to such a request. With every word recorded it is only too easy for one tactless remark to be taken out of context, while the existence of the recording may also inhibit witnesses or the free-flowing discussion that a constructive solution may need. You are within your rights to refuse such a request – unless your organisation's formal procedure makes explicit provision for tape recording.

A preparation check-list

Use the check-list on page 21 to ensure that you have thought of all the factors which may require decisions or arrangements before the interview.

Preparation check-list

1 Have all relevant witnesses been interviewed?

2 Will all necessary written statements be available?

3 Have these been copied to the employee?

4 Will all other relevant documentation be available:
   – attendance records
   – appraisal records
   – production or quality records
   – previous disciplinary records
   – relevant rules and regulations
   – other documentation (specify)?

5 Have you decided who else will attend the interview:
   – to present the management case
   – to keep notes
   – to give statements as witnesses?

6 Have you decided the general sequence or structure of the interview?

7 Have you notified the employee of the subject matter, time, date, location and nature of the interview?

8 Have all these details been confirmed in writing?

9 How much notice have you given the employee?

10 Is this sufficient for the employee to prepare a response?

11 Have you arranged for the interview to be held in a quiet and private setting?

12 Have you barred all interruptions?

13 Have you allowed adequate time for the interview?

14 Have you determined the form that a record of the interview should take?

3 conducting the interview: the procedure

The previous chapter included an outline of the sequence for a disciplinary interview as recommended by ACAS and many practitioners. In this chapter elements of this procedure will be examined in more detail. Emphasising the procedural aspects may give an impression of a very formal process – rather as if the interview equated to a hearing at an industrial tribunal. That is not the intention. A systematic approach is recommended not because formality is important for its own sake, but because it helps ensure thoroughness and fairness, and also that the interview achieves its objectives. In any event, the degree of formality will depend on:

- your organisation's disciplinary procedure. In the public sector, for example these procedures are often very detailed and may require the interview to be conducted by a formally designated disciplinary panel following a prescribed sequence. In other organisations the procedure may state no more than that a disciplinary interview will be held – leaving the format and process for individual managers to decide.

- the issue that has triggered the interview. A minor incident which, if proved, merits no more than a first verbal warning may be dealt with satisfactorily in a short, informal meeting between you and the employee. But an interview about a serious matter which may result in the employee's dismissal needs to be handled in a much more formal and systematic manner, particularly if the outcome may later be challenged by the employee on appeal or at an industrial tribunal.

Whatever the degree of formality, the conduct of the interview involves:

- an initial explanation of the status and purpose of the interview

- an explanation of the management complaint against the employee

- the employee's explanation

- questions about both of these explanations

- discussion about any other relevant matters

- a summary, highlighting key issues requiring decision

- the use of adjournments

- the announcement of your decision.

Initial explanation

Complications sometimes occur when managers fail to explain the status and purpose of the interview. They simply ask the employee to come and see them without saying why, and then talk about some incident that has caused them concern. The meeting may finish with the manager making a vague statement such as, 'I am sure you now understand the position.' If the same fault recurs the manager may then summon the employee and state that the matter is serious because 'this is the second time I have had to discipline you'. At this point the employee expresses surprise, and may obtain trade union backing to argue that the first discussion was not a disciplinary interview and that no formal warning has ever been given. Employers have lost tribunal cases because of this type of ambiguity.

If the requirement to attend the interview has been confirmed by a letter of the kind set out in the previous chapter, there should be no misunderstanding. Even here, though, it is advisable to open the interview by saying something like, 'As you know from my letter, this interview has been called in accordance with the company's disciplinary procedure. Can you just confirm that you understand this? Have you any queries about this before we start?' An opening statement confirming the status of the interview is even more important if it has been arranged only verbally.

There are also occasions when introductions need to be made before the interview proceeds, eg interviews for which you arrange the attendance of supporting managers, and where the employee is assisted by a colleague or trade union representative. You may start by saying 'So that we all know who's who, I shall be conducting this interview and I am Jane Smith, accounts manager. This is George Brown, accounts supervisor, who will be explaining the management's case, and this is Margaret Robinson, our departmental personnel officer, who is advising me on the company's disciplinary procedure and who will keep a note of the meeting. Would you please introduce your representative?'

The management case

To speak of 'the management case' may sound legalistic, but it is simply a shorthand phrase to describe the statement that you (or a manager who has conducted the preliminary enquiry) need to make to explain why the interview has been convened. Natural justice makes it essential that the employee understands why it has been decided that a disciplinary interview is necessary, and so hears the evidence which you have taken into account in deciding to convene the meeting.

It is a matter for decision (influenced by the requirements of your organisation's procedure) whether it is you who make this statement and call any witnesses, or whether this is done by another manager – perhaps the employee's immediate supervisor. In a simple case this may amount to little more than your making a statement such as this:

The matter I have to consider is the incident last week when I found you having an argument with a customer (name) *and heard you describe her as an interfering busybody. As you know, I had to*

Chartered Institute of Personnel and Development

Customer Satisfaction Survey

We would be grateful if you could spend a few minutes answering these questions and return the postcard to CIPD. <u>Please use a black pen to answer</u>. **If you would like to receive a free CIPD pen, please include your name and address.** IPD MEMBER Y/N

....

1. Title of book ....

2. Date of purchase: month ....   year ....

3. How did you acquire this book?
☐Bookshop   ☐Mail order   ☐Exhibition ☐Gift   ☐Bought from Author

4. If ordered by mail, how long did it take to arrive:
☐1 week   ☐2 weeks   ☐more than 2 weeks

5. Name of shop .... Town.. Country............

6. Please grade the following according to their influence on your purchasing decision with 1 as least influential: (please tick)

	1	2	3	4	5
Title					
Publisher					
Author					
Price					
Subject					
Cover					

7. On a scale of 1 to 5 (with 1 as poor & 5 as excellent) please give your impressions of the book in terms of: (please tick)

	1	2	3	4	5
Cover design					
Paper/print quality					
Good value for money					
General level of service					

8. Did you find the book:

Covers the subject in sufficient depth   ☐Yes   ☐No

Useful for your work   ☐Yes   ☐No

9. Are you using this book to help:
☐In your work ☐Personal study   ☐Both   ☐Other (please state)

Please complete if you are using this as part of a course

10. Name of academic institution..

11. Name of course you are following? ....

12. Did you find this book relevant to the syllabus? ☐Yes ☐No ☐Don't know

Thank you!

To receive regular information about CIPD books and resources call 020 8263 3387.

1795/05/00

2

Publishing Department

Chartered Institute of Personnel and Development

CIPD House

Camp Road

Wimbledon

London

SW19 4BR

intervene and give her an apology on behalf of the company. You went on a customer care course six months ago, and you must know the importance that the company places on treating all our customers with courtesy. But before I decide what action I might take, I want you to tell me what happened and why you behaved in this way.

In contrast, there can be very complex cases in which the explanation of the management's concerns involves hearing statements from several witnesses and the submission and explanation of extensive documentation. A typical case of this kind would involve a senior manager in a local authority or a construction company who is being 'charged' by his employer with negligence in handling complicated contractual matters. Here it is strongly advisable for you to chair the disciplinary hearing while another manager presents the results of what was probably a complex investigation.

The involvement of witnesses needs careful handling. The courts have made clear that when serious allegations against an employee are being made these statements should, if at all possible, be made personally at the disciplinary interview by those concerned, and the employee should have the opportunity to question these witnesses and put forward alternative evidence. As the manager convening the interview, you have to ensure the orderly conduct of witness statements and questioning. Remember:

● Witnesses should not sit in on the whole interview. They should be called in to give their evidence, be questioned, and then leave.

■ They should be restricted to giving relevant and factual evidence. A witness who begins to make irrelevant statements or allegations, or who tries to use the occasion to canvass personal opinions, should be stopped and required to keep to the point.

▲ When witnesses are being questioned – whether by the employee (or the employee's representative) or managers – you should try to restrict the process to genuine questioning. There is a tendency for questioners to start arguing with witnesses, or simply to make counter-statements.

The employee's explanation

The employee must be given an adequate opportunity to give his or her side of the story and to offer an explanation. When an employee is represented by a trade union official it is likely that most of this will be presented by the official, and it will probably be comprehensive. An employee who is unrepresented may find it difficult to present a coherent account in a logical and orderly sequence. Because the purpose of the interview is to discover the full truth – not to trap the employee – you must resist any temptation to take advantage of an employee's inability to describe events in a systematic manner. They should be advised in advance that the best plan is usually to give a straightforward, chronological account of the events in question, and then talk about anything which in their view helps to explain matters. You are not obliged to make employees' cases for them, but you should exercise patience in listening to what may be a rather muddled account. By asking questions, you should also ensure that they have covered everything they want to say. If an employee has witnesses, they should be extended the same care and courtesy as the management witnesses and, if necessary, given assurances that their support of the employee will not be held against them.

Questioning the explanations

When questioning the employee and any witnesses, the objective of getting at all the facts should be kept in mind. You may disagree with something they have said, but that is not necessarily a good reason for questioning it. Your objectives should be:

- to clarify statements rather than challenge them

- to use questions to ensure that you will have all the relevant facts when you come to make your decision.

The skills involved in questioning are dealt with in Chapter 4. Here it is sufficient to suggest that, as the interview proceeds, it is helpful to note (mentally or by jotting down a reminder) any gaps in the facts, or any ambiguities or generalisations that need clarification by any of the participants. In this connection, it is not only the employee who may need to be questioned. Supervisors and managers are just as likely to make statements that need to be clarified. Thus a supervisor may say that the employee 'has often been late during the past few months'. It is then for you to ask for details – how many times, how late, when, and why?

General discussion

In many disciplinary cases, facts are only part of the story: the organisational and emotional context is often of greater significance. The facts need to be established in the first, major part of the interview, but this can usefully be followed by a less formal discussion in which you explore attitudes, motivation, and contextual factors. The facts should show what the employee did, but you need also to consider why the employee behaved in this way. Although some indications will have been given by the employee's explanation, you should be sensitive to the possibility that other factors may exist that have not yet been identified. A check-list can help to ensure that you consider all the possible underlying causes (see the table on page 34). (See also Chapter 5 on mitigating circumstances.)

Summaries

It is very helpful, particularly if the interview has been long and complex, for both you and the employee to finish by summarising what each considers to be the key points. This helps to prevent misunderstandings about what the interview has been about, and can usefully form the basis for the interview record. The best plan is generally to ask the employee to summarise first. After the general discussion ends, you might say:

You've now given me your account of events and your explanation of how and why you behaved as you did. This has involved a lot of detail, and I want to be sure I understand what you feel are the most important aspects. It might help if you told me which key points you think I should take into account in making my decision.

The employee may have to repeat some things he or she has already said, but it is important to ensure that the employee has had every opportunity to explain his or her position. After the employee's summary you can end the interview by summarising what *you* feel are the key issues. For example, if the employee has allegedly made false claims for overtime payments, you might say:

Your supervisor has told us that last month you claimed, and were paid, for two hours' overtime each Friday evening, but that this time was not worked. We have looked at the overtime claim forms and you accept that you did make these claims but did not work the hours. You have explained this by saying that you made the claims to compensate for time spent on work you had taken home. You say your supervisor agreed to this, but he denies it. I will now adjourn the meeting for half an hour while I consider my decision.

Adjournments

This example illustrates that it is advisable to make a break between hearing the case and deciding what should be done. It may well be that you have reached a firm conclusion by the time you make your final summary. Even then it is better to have a short adjournment. This serves two purposes:

● It gives you time to reconsider the matter and make sure that your initial view has not been reached too hastily.

■ It demonstrates to the employee the matter is being considered carefully and will not be an instant and perhaps emotionally biased decision.

A break between the end of the interview and announcing your decision is not the only time at which an adjournment may be necessary. Other reasons may apply during the interview:

● Tempers may become frayed, or the employee may become upset and too emotional for the interview to proceed fairly. A short break can then be a helpful way of restoring a calmer atmosphere.

■ The employee (or representative) may unexpectedly raise issues that neither you nor any attending manager have adequate knowledge of. It is wholly in order, if this happens, to say that you need time to look into these new issues and will therefore adjourn while you do so. An adjournment of this kind may need to be for a day or more if the new matters require detailed investigation.

▲ It is not unusual for disciplinary interviews to take considerably more time than was first envisaged. You may then wish to continue, perhaps, into the evening. It is difficult, however, to sustain the attention that a complex case merits if the interview drags on for hour after hour. It is better to acknowledge that more time is needed and so adjourn, having set a time to resume and complete the interview.

Announcing your decision

The details of this final stage are considered in Chapter 6. It is sufficient here to note that in procedural terms this announcement should be:

 made as soon as possible after the interview discussion and summary have been concluded, provided you give yourself time to think through the issues and alternatives

■ very clearly described and explained.

On the first point, it is unsatisfactory to keep the employee in mental suspense about the outcome for any longer than is necessary. On the second point, it is vital for there to be no misunderstanding about this outcome. It is therefore advisable to explain your decision verbally, check that it has been understood, and confirm it in writing – preferably on the same day.

Discussion check-list

Ask yourself whether the employee's conduct might be explained (at least in part) by

- factors personal to that employee:
  - physical or mental ill-health
  - stress caused by outside work circumstances (eg domestic or financial worries)

- factors involving relationships at work:
  - personality clashes with supervisors or workmates
  - bullying, or racial or sexual harassment

- factors related to the job:
  - heavy working pressures
  - boredom or inactivity
  - incompatibility (ie the employee is in the wrong job)
  - physical factors (noise, dirt etc)
  - problems with equipment or materials

- factors related to terms and conditions:
  - pay (eg changes in bonus or overtime)
  - hours of work (eg unsocial hours, shift-working)

- factors related to supervision or training:
  - insufficient or poor-quality supervision
  - misunderstanding of supervisory instructions
  - inconsistent application of rules or regulations
  - inadequate training.

4 conducting the interview: the skills involved

Many of the concerns that managers have about conducting disciplinary interviews relate to doubts about their ability to keep control of the process, or fears that there may be later allegations of unfairness or discrimination. Particularly in serious cases, when dismissal is a possible outcome, the knowledge that you may eventually have to give evidence to an industrial tribunal about your conduct of the interview can inhibit what could otherwise have been a less tense and more productive meeting. These concerns are primarily about the skills involved rather than simply an understanding of procedural principles.

Conducting an effective disciplinary interview certainly requires a blend of skills which can all be developed and improved:

- chairing skills
- skill in handling anger or fear
- communication skills
- questioning skills
- counselling skills.

Chairing skills

The skills involved in chairing meetings are not of obvious relevance to the type of disciplinary interview that involves one manager talking over a simple incident in an informal manner with one employee. But as the previous chapters have explained, many interviews have to involve other managers, employees as witnesses, and the employee's trade union representative or colleague. The subject matter may also be complex, with all the risks involved of people giving confused accounts of what happened and of arguments developing about differences of interpretation or opinion. It is in these more complex cases that chairing skills become important. Effective chairmanship includes:

- ensuring that everyone understands the purpose of and the procedure for the meeting

- ensuring that any relevant documentation is introduced and explained at the right point in the proceedings

- keeping control – but in a facilitative, not domineering, manner

- pacing the meeting, ensuring that the discussion does not get bogged down on peripheral matters, and that adequate time is given to key issues

- ensuring that everyone (particularly the employee) leaves the meeting feeling that they have been able to say what they needed to

- using adjournments or changes of subject to prevent any discussion becoming overheated

- ensuring, through effective summaries, that when the interview concludes there is no misunderstanding about the key issues.

Skill in handling anger or fear

It is important throughout the interview that you avoid becoming emotionally involved. You may also need to defuse anger or reduce the employee's fear or tension.

Employees charged with a disciplinary offence may sometimes respond by making accusations of unfairness against you or other managers. They may challenge your statements, implying or stating that they consider you are biased or that the interview is simply a charade to justify action which you have already decided to take.

Accusations of this kind can be very hurtful, and it is natural that you should resent them. Yet if you allow yourself to be provoked into an emotional reaction the result may be to confirm in the employee's mind the very accusation that he or she has made. It can take considerable self-control to stay even-tempered, but this may be essential to the necessary perception of a fairly conducted interview. Some possible responses to provocative allegations are:

● 'I hear what you say, but I am not going to enter into an argument with you about it.'

■ 'I think, perhaps, you may reconsider that when you have had more time to give it thought. I want, now, to turn to another matter.'

▲ 'You have a right to your views, but you must not expect me necessarily to agree with them. Now let's move on.'

It can also be helpful to exercise patience rather than try to stop a flow of angry statements. Interruptions may only inflate the employee's sense of anger and frustration. Let the employee talk the anger out of their system. Pay attention, but do not respond. When the employee eventually falls silent, all that may be necessary in order to resume a more rational discussion is a simple, 'I understand. Now we need to talk about the next topic.'

Identifying anger is not generally a problem. What may be less obvious is the effect of fear and tension on employees' ability to express themselves clearly, or to tell you all you need to know. It is best to assume that any employee attending a disciplinary interview will be affected to some degree by worry about the outcome. So you need to bear in mind that the employee's ability to listen calmly and carefully to what you have to say may be severely impaired. An employee once told an industrial tribunal: 'I was so worried about losing my job that I didn't take in what the manager was telling me, and when I asked him to repeat it, he said he hadn't got time to say things twice.'

It is vital that the employee does understand what you have to say, and the onus for ensuring this lies on you. There are several ways of modifying the effect of tension:

● Do not keep the employee waiting in the outer office: start the interview as soon as the employee arrives.

■ Make sure that the employee and his or her representative or witnesses are seated comfortably and have somewhere to put their documents.

▲ Take time at the beginning of the interview to explain its purpose and procedure. Do so quietly and calmly and, if you know you are normally a quick speaker, try to slow down.

● Do not dramatise the occasion by emphasising its potentially serious outcome.

● Use a down-to-earth approach and stress that you will keep an open mind until you have heard everything that needs to be said.

● So far as possible, avoid interrupting the employee and keep any comments about what he or she says until the latter part of the interview.

■ Treat the employee with common courtesy and avoid making remarks that might be interpreted as intimidating or sarcastic.

▲ Avoid the use of managerial or technical jargon unless you are confident the employee uses the same terms.

Communication skills

Once the interview is under way its effectiveness is largely dependent on the key communication skills of explaining and listening. You will have points that you wish the employee to understand and respond to. You need equally to understand the employee's position – not just the words used, but the underlying attitudes and motivation. There are two common faults for managers:

● being so concerned with stating and explaining your own managerial concerns that you fail to listen attentively to what the employee has to say

■ failing to check that the employee has understood what you have said.

Remember, too, that communication is not just verbal. You may unwittingly convey messages about your attitude by the way you sit or gesture. Obvious examples include indicating impatience or disbelief by tapping a pencil on your desk, leaning back in your chair and looking away, or raising your eyebrows. The employee's posture and gestures may provide similar attitudinal clues.

Questioning skills

An important part of the communication process is the use of skilled questioning. Employees may be reluctant to talk about some aspects of the matter in hand or may have difficulty in expressing their views or concerns. You need to get the full picture – both from them and from any witnesses – and cannot rely simply on what they first choose to tell you. Questioning skills are needed, many of which are almost identical with those used in effective selection interviewing. Four main types of questions are involved.

The open-ended question

This is particularly useful in the early stages, when you are asking the employee or a witness to give their account of events. It gives no clue to the type of answer you expect, but simply asks them to tell their story. For example:

'What happened in the incident involving a customer last Friday?'

'What was said in the discussion you had with your supervisor yesterday?'

The probing or clarifying question

The answers to the initial open-ended questions may be inadequate or very general. You will need to probe into such responses. An example of a short sequence of questions illustrates this:

Open-ended question 'What happened in the incident with the customer?'

Answer 'I had a bit of an argument about her right to a refund.'

First probing question 'How did the argument start?'

Answer 'I told her she had to produce the receipt and she said she hadn't been given one.'

Second probing question 'What did you then say to her?'

If the answer to the last of these questions is along the lines of 'I told her we always gave receipts so she must be mistaken' then a useful, additional probing question would be, 'Tell me what you said: what were your actual words?' Asking employees and witnesses to repeat what was actually said during a discussion or confrontation, rather than accepting a less specific account, often throws valuable new light on the situation.

You may even have to use a role-playing approach to get at the truth. If, in the above example, there is still difficulty in discovering who said what, you might try this approach: 'Imagine I am the customer. I say to you, "I wasn't given a receipt." Now I want you to reply, just as you did when you had the argument.'

The closed question

Closed questions can be answered with a simple yes or no.

implies that, after you have established the facts, you
ider and discuss the measures that the employee and
might pursue to correct any failings that have emerged
e interview. The emphasis should be on positive action
e employee – to gain his or her commitment and sense
rsonal responsibility for achieving an improvement.
either dictating what should be done or simply
ing generalities. So the starting-point can be to ask
ployee, 'What do you think *you* should do to begin
g an improvement (or to avoid any repetition of the
m we have been discussing)?'

e the issue has been bad timekeeping, and a final
has to be given about the inevitability of dismissal if
no improvement. A traditional managerial approach,
any discussion, would be to set a limit such as 'If
ate by more than five minutes without good reason
than two occasions in the course of the next six
you will be dismissed.' A counselling approach would
ifferent. You would say something along these lines:

to issue a final warning because the matter has become
But I would be extremely disappointed if you had to be
nd I am sure you, too, want to prevent this. I think you
it helpful to set yourself a timekeeping target for
t. What do you think you should aim for in terms of
ping record over, say, the next six months?

then lead to a discussion and agreement between
e employee. The interesting point about this

They should be avoided while you are opening up the
interview, but can be useful to confirm single facts. Suppose,
for example, that in the example of the argument with the
customer the employee says, 'I thought she was trying to cheat
us and told her so', you might pose the closed question, 'Did
you actually use the word "cheat"?' Closed questions should
be used sparingly, and generally restricted to clarifying factual
issues.

The playback question

This is a variation on the closed question, because it may be
answered satisfactorily with a simple 'Yes.' It is used to play
back to the employee your understanding of what they have
said so as to check that this is correct. Some examples:

● 'Are you saying that you have never been told about the
company's overtime procedure?'

■ 'Would it be correct to summarise your explanation as …?'

▲ 'Am I right in assuming that the important point in your
mind was …?'

The time for most questions of this kind is towards the end
of the interview, when you need to be sure that you have
understood the employee's statements and views before you
consider what action to take.

There are three types of questions to be avoided: the multiple,
the leading, and the discriminatory question.

The multiple question

Impatience may lead to questions being asked that cover several different topics. For example: 'Tell me why you failed to report the problem to your supervisor and whether you said anything about it to any of your colleagues – or was it that you could not find anyone to talk to because of the lunch break?' The probability is that the employee will respond to only the last part of this multiple question, leaving the rest unanswered.

The leading question

The last part of the multiple question above is also a leading question. It invites the employee to agree with a possible explanation you have thought of, instead of probing for the employee's explanation. There is little point, either, in such leading questions as, 'You do agree, don't you, that it would have been better to have been more polite to the customer?' It would be a bold employee who would say no, and the obvious answer, 'Yes', will not throw much light on the situation.

The discriminatory question

Some employees in a disciplinary situation will be very sensitive to any implied race or sex discrimination, and interviewers need to be aware of this. Some research studies have indicated that women and ethnic minority employees tend to be subject to more rigorous disciplinary action than white men. Even if this is difficult to prove statistically,

subjective perceptions of bias can be as sign discrimination. You need to be very circumstances where such perceptions may asking questions in a way that might be ta an unfairly discriminatory attitude. This example, if the employee in the customer i woman and the customer a white man. 'Are you sure he understood what you we you know that men tend to make that joke?' may well be thought by the empl of a bias against someone speaking wit or against women.

Counselling skills

Even when formal disciplinary action are often cases in which this can be counselling approach. There will al evident that no disciplinary outcom but the employee needs advice an improve their conduct or performa most cases, the best outcome of that the employee remains in en fully satisfactory member of the v will be cases where dismissal is n and a wilful failure to heed tolerated. But that should no setting improvement, rather th disciplinary objective.

This con you at th by th of pe Avoi preac the e makin proble

Suppos warnin there is without you are on more months, be very d

I have had so serious. dismissed, would find improveme your timeke

This could you and t

approach is that employees often commit themselves to tougher targets than you might impose. Indeed, you may even have to caution them about being too optimistic about their rate of improvement. But once they have made a commitment they 'own' it and will be far more likely to work hard to deliver it than if you had imposed a target.

There is another point. Further disciplinary action after failing to meet an imposed target may be resented on the grounds that the target was unrealistic. This reaction cannot be sustained if the target was suggested by the employee.

So the primary skill in this, as in other forms of counselling, is to encourage the employee to take ownership of the corrective action – not to solve the situation for them. There may, of course, be measures only you can take, such as arranging attendance at a training course. Even then, however, you should encourage the employee to identify the personal objectives for which the training is provided, to suggest targets to aim for (eg in performance) and to commit themselves to supportive action, such as keeping a learning log.

The employee's commitment to an improvement programme can be reinforced by agreeing a clear set of time-limited objectives, linked to a review process. Make clear, however, that these review meetings will not be a continuation of the disciplinary interview: they will constitute progress sessions at which you will jointly consider how well things are going and what further improvement may be needed. Once a satisfactory standard has been reached, the employee's further performance can be assessed within the normal performance appraisal process.

In some instances the problem leading to the disciplinary interview will be something unrelated to work, such as health or domestic matters. It may not then be wise for you to attempt to give the necessary advice. There are great dangers in trying to act the amateur psychologist or marriage guidance counsellor. What you can do in such cases is help the employee contact the right source of professional assistance. Most organisations' personnel departments keep lists of relevant external contacts (such as Relate), many can refer health matters to their occupational physician, while some offer confidential counselling services as an employee benefit. Make full use of any such facilities if the matter is one outside your own area of expertise.

5 deciding what should be done

Once the facts of the case have been explained and discussed, the major part of the interview will be over – at least in terms of the time involved. But the most important element, the outcome, has still to be decided. It is always advisable to give yourself time to think about this. It may be for no more than a few minutes, but in complex cases a much longer adjournment may be needed. You may, for example, want to consult a senior manager or obtain further advice from your personnel manager before reaching a decision.

Be wary, though, of consulting your senior manager if he or she is the person to whom the employee has a right of appeal against your decision. The courts have made clear that for the principles of natural justice to be met, the manager hearing an appeal should not have had any prior involvement with the case.

As for the case itself, there are six main stages to consider:

1   weighing up the facts: considering both sides of the story

2   taking account of any mitigating circumstances

3   relating the case to your organisation's values, standards, and precedents

4   distinguishing between conduct and competence

5   looking at the employee's record

6   considering the alternatives.

Weighing up the facts

If the employee does not dispute any of the facts about the case you can rapidly move to the next stage. Unfortunately this is often not the case. The employee will tell one story, a supervisor or witnesses will give another. Your task is to weigh up what you have heard in a dispassionate manner and decide which account you should place greater weight on.

It is important to note that in the employment context the law does not expect an employer to reach a conclusion 'beyond reasonable doubt' (the criminal law test). You are entitled to reach a common-sense view on the balance of probabilities – provided you do so in an unbiased manner in the light of information obtained after an adequate investigation.

Mitigating circumstances

It may be evident that the employee is at fault and that, as a matter of general principle, the offence merits formal disciplinary action. Before you decide what the appropriate sanction should be, consider whether there are any aspects that would justify moderating the normal penalty. Typical mitigating circumstances are:

- the employee's inexperience – a new employee, or an employee who has very recently transferred to a new job, may not yet have adjusted to the expected standards of conduct or performance

- ill health or stress – whether or not this is related to work

- unusual working pressures, such as having worked continuously over a double shift just before carelessness or an altercation with a customer occurred

- provocation, such as racial abuse or bullying by workmates or a supervisor

- inadequate explanation of rules or procedures by the supervisor

- inconsistent enforcement of regulations or standards, eg a no-smoking rule that is strictly applied by some supervisors and not at all by others

- misunderstanding of instructions caused by language difficulties – a particular risk with some ethnic minority employees unless their supervisors are sensitive to the need for effective communication.

In most cases in which one or other of such factors is apparent there will be a need for some form of counselling. Note, too, that a review of mitigating circumstances may indicate that corrective action is needed by other staff as well as by the employee. Supervisors, for example, may need to be given clearer guidance about their responsibilities, or coached to improve their people management skills.

Your organisation's values, standards, and precedents

Acceptable standards of conduct or performance in one organisation may differ from those in another. You need to set your decision in the context of your own organisation's culture – its core values, the standards it sets for quality and conduct, and the expectations of managers and staff created by precedent.

It is important that you do not assess a case simply by reference to the standards that you would like to see upheld, unless these coincide with those of the organisation at large. Cases have been lost at industrial tribunals when individual managers have used the disciplinary process to introduce stricter personal controls or higher standards than the organisation has set or maintained corporately. The dismissed employees have been able to argue that other employees have not been disciplined for the same conduct and that these differences of disciplinary standards have consequently been unfair.

Consider, as an example, a factory employee who has been discovered taking home scrap material without permission. You would need to consider these questions:

- Have clear instructions been issued to employees about the procedure for obtaining permission to take scrap?

- Are employees regularly reminded of these instructions? Or were these issued many years ago, perhaps before the employee concerned was taken on?

- Have these instructions been consistently enforced? Or has unofficial custom and practice eroded their application?

- Have there been previous disciplinary cases for taking scrap? If so, how have they been dealt with?

In the example of an employee who has been rude to a customer, there are similar questions to consider:

- Has a high standard of customer relations been promoted throughout the workforce as one of the organisation's core values?

- Have employees been given any training about how to respond to aggressive or confused customers?

- Has the particular employee had such training?

- What example has been set by the employee's supervisor?

You may also need to consider standards specific to particular types of job. For example, minor dishonesty (eg in claiming expenses) may well need to be treated as a major matter for an employee such as a cashier, who is in a position of trust.

The same offence might merit less serious action for an employee in a job where accountability for money is not a factor.

The general principle is that the right course of action should be related to your organisation's formally promulgated standards, and consistent with any well-established custom and practice.

Conduct and competence

It is clearly unfair to discipline employees for not doing something for which they lack the necessary competence. The remedies in such cases include training or transfers to other work they are able to perform – not disciplinary sanctions. But distinguishing between conduct and competence is not always easy. Take a production worker who has had the normal training but produces a consistently higher proportion of faults than other staff. What is the reason? It might be continual carelessness, which would make it a matter of conduct; or it might be caused by an inherent lack of some necessary aptitude, a matter of competence.

The right action in cases of this kind depends on your making the correct analysis of the underlying cause. The distinction is reflected in the statutory and case law principle governing unfair dismissal, which require employers to specify whether a dismissal has been on grounds of 'capability' (ie competence) or conduct. Conduct includes many different forms of unacceptable behaviour, such as being abusive, continual lateness, absenteeism, refusing to comply with reasonable instructions, or falsifying expense claims. The tribunals accept that dismissal for incapability may sometimes be fair – say, when no suitable alternative job is available. But they also require the employer to be specific about this and to state clearly whether a dismissal was for misconduct or incapability. Confusing these two causes, particularly by treating incapability as misconduct, may make a dismissal unfair.

The employee's record

The employee's past history with the organisation may have a major influence on a decision about the correct course of action, and you should always take this into account. The most obvious situation is that of an employee who repeats a serious offence after being issued with a formal warning. Provided you are sure the offence occurred, and unless there are very strong mitigating circumstances, you will normally have little option but to impose whatever sanction the earlier warning implied.

It is particularly important that unambiguous written final warnings are shown to mean what they say. If an employee has received a written warning to the effect 'Any repetition of this conduct during the next 12 months will result in your dismissal' then dismissal should follow if the offence is repeated a few months later (provided the fact of repetition has been established by a proper investigation and interview). Failure to act on formal warnings brings such warnings into disrepute.

There will be other situations, however, that are far less clear-cut. You need to consider not only the disciplinary record but also the quality of the whole of the employee's past service. This may involve looking at attendance and appraisal records and talking to the employee's current or previous supervisors. Consider these questions:

- How long is the employee's service?

- What has been the general standard of the employee's conduct and performance over this period?

- Has the employee's behaviour changed recently and, if so, why?

- Have there been any previous similar complaints about the employee? If so, how were they dealt with?

How seriously you deal with an offence may then be influenced by the general record. One lapse of conduct that is wholly out of character with the general behaviour of an otherwise satisfactory employee should be treated differently from the same lapse committed by a short-service employee who has given previous cause for concern.

Alternative courses of action

Having heard the case and considered all the factors outlined in this chapter, you have now to decide the appropriate action. Try not to be influenced by what may have been your initial view. It is all too easy to start an interview with the thought that there has been a potential cause for dismissal, and thus to allow dismissal to dominate the way you consider the case. It is much better to run through a check-list of the possible courses of action, making sure that you could give a sound reason why any that you discard would not be appropriate. These include:

● taking no action at all, ie dropping the case. The interview may have convinced you either that the whole case has been based on misunderstandings or that whatever has been alleged did not, in fact, occur. In such cases it is a strength, not a weakness, to close the matter, provided you explain your conclusion. You may need to assure the employee that no adverse record will be held on file, and to counsel any supervisor who made the initial complaint.

■ deciding on some form of non-disciplinary corrective action. This may involve counselling, training, or, in the case of ill-health, reference to your organisation's medical adviser.

▲ taking no formal disciplinary action, but setting or agreeing targets for improvement. This can apply particularly to cases of poor performance and unsatisfactory attendance. It is a particularly suitable course of action for the inexperienced employee whose faults may have included an element of carelessness, though not so far as to be considered misconduct. It can be made clear that failure to reach the standards set might result in formal disciplinary action, but that the current target-setting will not be recorded as a disciplinary measure.

- giving an informal verbal reprimand. First and minor offences may not merit formal disciplinary action, although the employee needs to be told that the conduct involved is unsatisfactory. With young employees in particular this approach, combined with counselling, can be far more effective in achieving an improvement than heavy-handed, formal sanctions.

- a verbal, but recorded, warning. Although this may sound like a contradiction in terms, its use as a minor, semi-formal disciplinary measure is well established. The employee is told that a formal, written warning will not be issued, but a note will be kept that an interview was necessary and a specified improvement is being sought. Note that this low-level warning does not meet the criterion of the first written warning, which constitutes the initial formal stage of most organisations' disciplinary procedures.

- formal, written warnings. It is a basic principle of fair practice – as well as of employment case law and ACAS advice – that an employee should not normally be dismissed unless there has been a prior written warning (or warnings). There is an exception (summary dismissal for gross misconduct) but this must be reserved for extremely serious cases (see below). In most cases in which formal disciplinary action is justified you will need to consider the issue of a formal, written warning and to check your organisation's disciplinary procedure about this:

O What does the procedure state about the issue of such warnings? For example, do you have the authority to issue them without reference to your senior manager or personnel manager?

☐ Must they be in a prescribed form? Is there a standard letter?

△ Does the procedure require at least two such warnings (a first and then a final warning) before dismissal?

O Alternatively, does it allow you to move straight to a final warning (ie without a previous warning) in serious cases which fall just short of gross misconduct?

O Does the procedure require written warning to be disregarded after a defined period?

Whatever the precise form of a written warning, it should always be accompanied by an explanation of the desired improvement, together with details of any targets, time limits and reviews. The primary purpose of a warning is to prevent later and more serious action having to be taken – not to make it easier to implement a later dismissal, even though this is one effect of the warning process.

Dismissal

A decision to dismiss is always a serious matter. It may seem the obvious outcome of a disciplinary interview in which the employee's conduct has been shown to be wholly unacceptable, and for which he or she has been unwilling to accept either blame or a need to improve. Even then, it is always worth giving yourself time to think through the issues listed above, and to make your decision quietly and calmly. The two situations in which dismissal is the right option are:

- when the employee is subject to a final, written warning, has made little or no attempt to meet the requirements of that warning, has repeated the conduct that the warning stated would result in dismissal, and there are no mitigating circumstances.

- when the employee is guilty of gross misconduct, whether or not he or she is subject to a previous warning. The only legal definition of gross misconduct is conduct that goes to the root of the employment contract – which is not of great practical help. Case law has however shown that gross misconduct includes, as examples,

  - serious physical assault on another employee

  - stealing the employer's or another employee's property

  - falsifying claims for payments

  - serious breaches of safety rules, resulting in risk of injury or death

- O blatant and persistent refusal to comply with reasonable instructions

- O being at work under the influence of alcohol or drugs

- ☐ serious breaches of confidentiality (such as passing commercially sensitive information to a competitor).

These are only examples. In reality, you have to exercise good judgement, case by case, and ask yourself: 'Was the employee's conduct so bad that no reasonable employer could be expected, in our particular circumstances, to allow the employee to continue in employment?' The factors involved in your organisation must influence your decision. For example, if the employee works in an environment in which smoking is banned because of a high risk of fire or explosion, a breach of the no-smoking rule may well constitute gross misconduct. The same breach in a no-smoking office may merit no more than a verbal rebuke.

The terms 'summary dismissal' or 'dismissal without notice' are often applied to dismissals for gross misconduct. Managers sometimes think this implies that employees can be dismissed the instant that misconduct is discovered. This is not so. There is *always* a need for a disciplinary investigation and a disciplinary interview. The right course of action is generally to suspend the employee (on normal pay) while the investigation is conducted, require him or her to come in to attend the interview, and only then (provided the case is established) dismiss without notice.

Suspension and fines

Suspension without pay is sometimes used as a disciplinary sanction, but only if it is specifically provided for in employees' contracts of employment. Without this provision, the stopping of pay will constitute a breach of contract and probably, too, a breach of the Wages Act 1986.

It is similarly a potential breach of contract and statute law to deduct money from wages as some form of fine or payment for damaged work or lost cash or property. There are some statutory exceptions in the Wages Act for employees in the retail trade, but this is not a sanction open to general use. In any event, the concept of 'punishment' is not normally helpful. As stated throughout this book, in almost all cases the emphasis should be on securing improvement.

6 announcing your decision

The disciplinary interview is not complete until you have announced and explained your decision. How this decision is announced is an important part of the whole process. Done well, it can be the first step towards remotivating the employee and achieving the required improvement. Handled badly, it may cause misunderstanding or generate resentment. There are four main elements:

1   Tell the employee what your decision is regarding the formal disciplinary situation.

2   If provided for in your organisation's procedure, explain the employee's appeal rights.

3   Explain the objectives for the future and, if appropriate, agree targets and supportive action.

4   Confirm the whole position in writing.

The disciplinary decision

A formal disciplinary interview is a serious matter and may be the first step on the road to a dismissal. To avoid any misunderstanding and to provide a record which may become important at a later stage, the nature and formal status of your decision must be unambiguous. You should also announce this as soon as you reconvene after any adjournment. The employee will be in a state of suspense, wondering what the outcome will be. In this state, he or she will be unlikely to absorb any lengthy preliminary comments, just wanting to know if you have decided to apply any disciplinary sanctions. It is best, too, to be very straightforward in your announcement, even if you feel uncomfortable about being so blunt. The time to talk about a constructive way forward is after you have stated the formal decision – not before. To illustrate this, compare these two opening statements:

I have found this a difficult case to decide. You have admitted that what you did was wrong but have also complained about a lack of direction from your supervisor. We certainly need to make sure it doesn't happen again; I'm afraid that if it does, things may become more serious. But in the meantime, I'm sure I can rely on you to do your best to prevent this happening.

I have considered very carefully everything you have told me, but I have decided that the matter cannot be overlooked. I will therefore be issuing you with a first, formal, written warning. This will state that if there is any repetition of your conduct during the next 12 months, you will be liable to be issued with a formal, final, written warning. If there is no repetition during this period, this first warning will be disregarded. Do you understand?

The first example sounds much less harsh than the second, but what does it mean in formal disciplinary terms? Does it constitute a formal warning? What does the phrase 'things may become more serious' imply? The employee may interpret the whole statement as no more than a mild verbal rebuke, whereas in the manager's mind it may have been intended as a serious warning.

The second example is unambiguous. The employee's conduct has been assessed as unacceptable and a first written warning will be issued. The duration of the warning and what will happen if it is ignored have also been stated. Finally, the employee has been asked if this has all been understood. Everything is clear. This may seem harsh, but it is far more important to ensure clarity than to soften the blow by using imprecise terms which may only result in later disagreement as to what was intended.

Appeal rights

Immediately after announcing your formal decision, you should remind the employee of any appeal rights provided for in your organisation's procedure. As noted earlier, many organisations restrict appeals to dismissal, although a number extend this to final warnings. It is far less common for appeals to apply to earlier warnings. If appeal rights exist, another very clear statement should follow the announcement of your decision, eg:

If you wish to appeal against my decision, you must write to the chief executive, giving your reasons, within the next five working days.

Employees sometimes challenge a decision immediately, and begin to repeat arguments they used during the main part of the interview. It is a mistake to be drawn into an argument or further discussion at this point. You need to be very firm about this and close the interview quickly to prevent the situation deteriorating.

Explaining future objectives

Assuming you have not had to close the interview to prevent an argument, you can now move on to the more constructive aspects, eg something along these lines:

I have explained the formal position: now we need to consider how you can ensure that we never have to meet like this again. I will be delighted if in due course we are able to disregard the warning. What ideas do you have about what you can do to ensure we achieve this success?

It is at this stage that counselling skills become important. The employee's morale and self-regard will normally have suffered a severe knock by being subjected to formal disciplinary action. Now is the time to begin the process of recovery. In addition to agreeing targets for improvements in conduct, attendance, or performance you may also wish to explain the importance you and your organisation place on the maintenance of certain values and standards. The employee (as well as you) needs to set the incident that triggered the disciplinary action within the broad context of your organisation's aims and culture. The disciplined employee needs to think of the future in terms of rejoining the team rather than of being labelled a potential outcast.

Confirming the decision

The outcome of the interview should always be confirmed in writing. Whereas this is an obvious necessity if the decision has been to issue a written warning, its importance is not always realised if the outcome was to take no further action or else to initiate non-disciplinary action. The employee who, as a result of the disciplinary interview, has been found to be blameless deserves a written confirmation of this conclusion. Similarly, when other, non-disciplinary action is the outcome, it is helpful to write and explain what this is. When formal warnings are issued, the first part of the letter should be in the same unambiguous terms as your verbal announcement, eg:

This letter confirms the decision I announced at the conclusion of the disciplinary interview yesterday. I decided that your conduct (give brief details) had been unacceptable and that you would therefore be issued with a first, formal, written warning in accordance with the company's disciplinary procedure. This letter constitutes that warning. Should there be any repetition of your conduct during the next 12 months you will be liable to receive a second and final written warning. If there is no repetition during this period this current warning will be disregarded...

The letter can go on to set out anything that has been agreed regarding improvement targets and reviews eg:

I also explained that I hoped very much that no further disciplinary action would become necessary. We discussed action you could take to ensure this and agreed that you would aim to (details of any improvement targets). I will also arrange for you to attend the next company one-day course on (details) *and to meet you to discuss your progress in three months' time.*

If you decide on dismissal, you would be well advised to take professional personnel or legal advice about the drafting of the dismissal letter because the precise wording – particularly about notice or notice pay and the last day of employment – can be of great importance. However, this is outside the scope of this book.

key points

- Be aware of the potential pitfalls, but make full use of the opportunities for setting high standards and achieving improvements in conduct and performance

- Know the details of your organisation's disciplinary policy and procedure.

- Prepare thoroughly: get the facts and relevant documents, decide whom to involve, inform the employee, allow adequate time, and ensure privacy and confidentiality.

- Ensure that the interview follows a logical and systematic sequence, starting with the facts, opening into discussion, and concluding with summaries.

- Ensure that the employee has every opportunity to give his or her side of the story.

- Use adjournments to restore a calm atmosphere, to investigate any new matters, and to give yourself time to think about outcomes.

- Recognise the skills needed: effective chairmanship, dealing with anger or fear, effective communication (telling and listening), skilful questioning, and constructive counselling.

- Avoid being drawn into arguments; keep your cool.

(continued overleaf)

- Do not try to trap the employee or exploit any difficulties he or she may have in explaining his or her side of the story.

- When considering a decision, do not jump to conclusions: weigh up all the facts and think through all the alternatives.

- Check whether there are mitigating circumstances.

- Ensure that your decision is consistent with your organisation's values, standards, and precedents.

- Consider the employee's record.

- Be ready to drop the matter if no further action is justified.

- Consider the value of non-disciplinary action: training, coaching, and counselling.

- Agree targets for improvement and set review dates; encourage the employee to suggest what these targets should be.

- Check your organisation's disciplinary rules regarding the nature, use, and issue of formal disciplinary sanctions.

- When announcing formal sanctions (eg formal warnings), do so in direct and unambiguous terms.

- Ensure that you understand the principles involved in summary dismissals for gross misconduct, and do not dismiss on this basis without prior investigation and a disciplinary interview.

- Do not use suspension without pay unless this is provided for in employees' contracts.

- Always confirm the outcome of disciplinary interviews in writing.

further study

Reading

ACAS. *Discipline at Work*. London, Advisory, Conciliation and Arbitration Service, 1987.
An essential text on the handling of discipline. Industrial tribunals refer to its code and model procedures when assessing whether a dismissal is fair.

GREENHALGH R. *Industrial Tribunals*. 2nd edn, London, IPD, 1995.
This book (in the *Law and Employment* series) gives detailed guidance on the procedures and the process of preparing and presenting a case.

JAMES P. *and* LEWIS D. *Discipline*. London, IPM, 1992.
Also in the *Law and Employment* series, this provides an authoritative account of every aspect of discipline from both legal and good-practice viewpoints.

IDS. *Unfair Dismissal*. London, Incomes Data Services, 1993.
This is a useful source of reference about what constitutes fair and unfair disciplinary procedures, and includes summaries of tribunal and court cases that involved issues related to the conduct of disciplinary interviews and appeals.

SUMMERFIELD J. *and* VAN OUDTSHOORN L. *Counselling in the Workplace*. London, IPD, 1995.

A practical guide to counselling from setting up sound practice to devising counselling-skills training programmes.

WEIGHTMAN J. *Managing Human Resources*. 2nd edn. London, IPM, 1993.

A succinct general text about people management, with a brief but helpful final chapter on 'dealing with problem people'.

Training videos

BBC. *Successful Interviewing, Volumes 2 and 3*.

These videos show examples of good and bad disciplinary interviewing. Volume 2 covers 'Appraisals, Information-gathering, and Disciplinary Interviews'. Volume 3 covers 'Counselling, and Confrontational and Dismissal Interviews'.

VIDEO ARTS. *I'd Like a Word with You*.

This uses humour and serious information to illustrate the pitfalls of bad interviewing and the principles of the effective disciplinary interview.

Other titles in the *Management Shapers* series:

The Appraisal Discussion

Terry Gillen

The Appraisal Discussion shows you how to make appraisal a productive and motivating experience for all levels of performer – and help your credibility in the process! Practical advice is given on:

- ● assessing performance fairly and accurately

- ■ using feedback, including constructive criticism and targeted praise, to improve performance

- ▲ handling 'difficult' appraisees

- ● encouraging and supporting reluctant appraisees

- ● setting, and gaining commitment to, worthwhile objectives

- ● avoiding common appraiser problems from inadvertent bias to 'appraisal speak'

- ■ identifying ways to develop appraisees so they add value to the organisation.

First Edition
96 pages
Pbk
0 85292 751 7
1998
£5.95

Asking Questions

Ian MacKay

Asking Questions will help you ask the 'right' questions, using the correct form to elicit a useful response. All managers need to hone their questioning skills, whether interviewing, appraising or simply exchanging ideas. This book offers guidance and helpful advice on:

- using various forms of open questions – including probing, simple interrogative, opinion-seeking, hypothetical, extension and precision etc.

- encouraging and drawing out speakers through supportive statements and interjections

- establishing specific facts through closed or 'direct' approaches

- avoiding counter-productive questions

- using questions in a training context.

Second Edition
96 pages
Pbk
0 85292 768 1
November 1998
£5.95

Assertiveness

Terry Gillen

Assertiveness will help you feel naturally confident, enjoy the respect of others and easily establish productive working relationships, even with 'awkward' people. It covers:

- understanding why you behave as you do and, when that behaviour is counter-productive, knowing what to do about it

- understanding other people better

- keeping your emotions under control

- preventing others bullying, flattering or manipulating you against your will

- acquiring easy-to-learn techniques that you can use immediately

- developing your personal assertiveness strategy.

First Edition
96 pages
Pbk
0 85292 769 X
November 1998
£5.95

Constructive Feedback

Roland and Frances Bee

Constructive Feedback plays a vital role in enhancing performance and relationships. The authors help you identify when to give feedback, how best to give it, and how to receive and use feedback yourself. They offer sound, practical advice on:

- distinguishing between 'destructive' criticism and 'constructive' feedback

- using feedback to manage better – as an essential element of coaching, counselling, training and motivating your team

- improving your skills by following the 10 Tools of Giving Constructive Feedback

- dealing with challenging situations and people

- eliciting the right feedback to highlight your strengths and opportunities for your own development.

First Edition
96 pages
Pbk
0 85292 752 5
1998
£5.95

Leadership Skills

John Adair

Leadership Skills will give you confidence, guide and inspire you on your journey from being an effective manager to becoming a leader of excellence. Acknowledged as a world authority on leadership, Adair offers stimulating insights on:

- recognising and developing your leadership qualities

- acquiring the personal authority to give positive direction and the flexibility to embrace change

- acting on the key interacting needs – to achieve your task, build your team and develop its members

- transforming the core leadership functions such as planning, communicating and motivating, into practical skills you can master.

First Edition
96 pages
Pbk
0 85292 764 9
November 1998
£5.95

Listening Skills

Ian MacKay

Listening Skills describes techniques and activities to improve your ability and makes clear why effective listening is such a crucial management skill – and yet so often overlooked or neglected. Clear explanations will help you:

- recognise the inhibitors to listening

- improve your physical attention so you are seen to be listening

- listen to what is really being said by analysing and evaluating the message

- ask the right questions so you understand what is not being said

- interpret tone of voice and non-verbal signals.

Second Edition
96 pages
Pbk
0 85292 754 1
1998
£5.95

Making Meetings Work

Patrick Forsyth

Making Meeting Work will maximise your time – both before and during meetings – clarify your aims, improve your own and others' performance and make the whole process rewarding and productive – never frustrating and futile. The book is full of practical tips and advice on:

- drawing up objectives and setting realistic agendas

- deciding the who, where and when to meet

- chairing effectively – encouraging discussion, creativity and sound decision-making

- sharpening your skills of observation, listening and questioning to get across your points

- dealing with problem participants

- handling the follow-up – turning decisions into action.

First Edition
96 pages
Pbk
0 85292 765 7
November 1998
£5.95

Motivating People

Iain Maitland

Motivating People will help you maximise individual and team skills to achieve personal, departmental and, above all, organisational goals. It provides practical insights on:

- becoming a better leader and co-ordinating winning teams

- identifying, setting and communicating achievable targets

- empowering others through simple job improvement techniques

- encouraging self-development, defining training needs and providing helpful assessment

- ensuring pay and workplace conditions make a positive contribution to satisfaction and commitment.

First Edition
96 pages
Pbk
0 85292 766 5
November 1998
£5.95

Negotiating, Persuading and Influencing

Alan Fowler

Negotiating, Persuading and Influencing will help you develop
the critical skills you need to manage your staff effectively,
bargain successfully with colleagues or deal tactfully with
superiors – thus ensuring that a constructive negotiation
process leads to a favourable outcome. Sound advice and
practical guidance is given on:

- recognising and using sources of influence

- probing and questioning techniques to discover the other
  person's viewpoint

- adopting collaborative or problem-solving approaches

- timing your tactics and using adjournments

- conceding and compromising to find common ground

- resisting manipulative ploys

- securing and implementing agreement.

First Edition
96 pages
Pbk
0 85292 755 X
1998
£5.95

The Selection Interview

Penny Hackett

The Selection Interview will ensure you choose better people – more efficiently. It provides step-by-step guidance on techniques and procedures from the initial decision to recruit through to the critical final choice. Helpful advice is included on:

- drawing up job descriptions, employee specifications and assessment plans

- setting up the interview

- using different interview strategies and styles

- improving your questioning and listening skills

- evaluating the evidence to reach the best decision.

First Edition
96 pages
Pbk
0 85292 756 8
1998
£5.95

Working in Teams

Alison Hardingham

Working in Teams looks at teamworking from the inside. It will give you invaluable insights into how you can make a more positive and effective contribution – as team member or team leader – to ensure your team works together and achieves together. Clear and practical guidelines are given on:

- understanding the nature and make-up of teams

- finding out if your team is on track

- overcoming the most common teamworking problems

- recognising your own strengths and weaknesses as a team member

- giving teams the tools, techniques and organisational support they need.

First Edition
96 pages
Pbk
0 85292 767 3
November 1998
£5.95